Preface.
WHY THIS LITTLE BOOK.

About ten years ago the idea of writing a little cook book had its birth. We were in Almora that summer. Almora is a station far up in the Himalayas, a clean little bazaar nestles at the foot of enclosing mountains. Dotting the deodar-covered slopes of these mountains are the picturesque bungalows of the European residents, while towering above and over all are the glistening peaks of the eternal snows.

We love to think of this particular summer, for Lilavate Singh was with us. The thought of her always brings help and inspiration.

One day she prepared for the crowd of us a tiffin of delicious Hindustani food. That afternoon while we were sitting under the shade and fragrance of the deodar trees, we praised the tiffin. Before we knew it we were planning a cook book. It was to be a joint affair of Hindustani and English dishes, and Miss Singh was to be responsible for the Hindustani part of it. Our enthusiasm grew. For three or four days we talked of nothing else. We experimented, we planned; we dreamed, we wrote. But alas! other things soon thrust themselves upon us, and our unfinished cook book was pigeon-holed for years and years.

And it is not now what it would have been if finished then.

Many of the recipes, however, are those that Miss Singh gave us then. Some of them she might not recognize, for they have become quite Americanized, but they are hers nevertheless, and I hope that you will not only try them and enjoy them, but that they will help you to solve some of the problems of living and giving which are confronting us all these days.

I have told this story before, but it fits in well here. A lady in India once had an ayah, who from morning until night sang the same sad song as she would wheel the baby in its little go-cart up and down the mandal or driveway; as she would energetically jump it up and down; as she would lazily pat it to sleep, always and ever she could be heard chanting plaintively, "Ky a ke waste, Ky a ke waste, pet ke waste, pet ke waste."

The lady's curiosity was aroused. The words were simple enough, but they had no sense: "For why? For why? For why? For stomach! For stomach! For stomach!" wailed the ayah.

Desiring to know what was for why, and what was for stomach one day, the lady called the ayah to her and sought the interpretation thereof.

"This is the meaning, Oh mem sahiba," said the ayah: "Why do we live? What is the meaning of our existence? To fill our stomachs, to fill our stomachs."

You may smile at this and feel sorry for the poor benighted Hindu, who has such a low ideal of the meaning of life, but after all we cannot ignore the fact that we must eat, and that much as we dislike to acknowledge it, we are compelled to think a great deal about filling our stomachs. This is especially true these days, when prices have soared and soared and taken along with them, far out of the reach of many of us, certain articles of food which we heretofore have always felt were quite necessary to us.

The missionary on furlough is naturally regarded as a bureau of information regarding the land where he has lived and worked. Many are the questions asked. These questions are inclusive of life and experience in general, but in particular they are regarding the food. "What do you eat there? Do you get meat there? What kind of vegetables grow there? What about the fruit of India? Why don't missionaries do their own cooking? Do the cooks there cook well? Aren't you always glad to get back to the food in America?" These and similar questions are sure to be asked the missionary and others who have lived in foreign countries.

Feeling sure that everybody wants to know these very things about India, it might be well just here to answer some of these questions.

In regard to the meat in India: The Hindus are vegetarians, but the Mohammedans are great meat eaters. So are the English. Meat can be had almost every place. The kind of meat differs much in locality. Chickens can be obtained anywhere. The Indian cock is small of head and long of leg, shrill of voice and bold in spirit. The Indian hen is shy and wild, but gives plenty of small, delicately-flavored eggs. On the whole, aside from a few idiosyncrasies, the Indian fowl is very satisfactory.

In large cities like Bombay, Calcutta, Lucknow, Madras, etc., where there is a large English population, any kind of meat may be obtained. In other places only goat meat can be obtained. This is especially true in many hill stations. Even in small places, if there happens to be a large Mohammedan population, good beef and mutton can be obtained in the cold weather, and in many larger places where there are few Mohammedans no meat of any kind is to be found excepting chicken, and one usually has to raise them himself.

Meat is cheap in India. Indeed, in some places beef can be bought for two cents a pound. However, it is not so good as is the beef in America. In the hot weather, as it has to be eaten almost as soon as it is killed, it is tough and tasteless.

Vegetables differ, too, according to the locality. If Mrs. A, returned missionary from India, pathetically states that year in and year out she never gets *any* home vegetables, and thereby causes everybody to pity her, and if Mrs. B, returned missionary from India, boasts that she gets plenty of home vegetables, even better than she could get in America, and thereby causes everybody to envy her, don't think that either Mrs. A or Mrs. B have fibbed. Mrs. B lives up north and Mrs. A lives south, and both speak truthfully.

The same is true in regard to fruits. Certain fruits, such as the citrus fruits, the unexcelled mango, bananas, etc., are found all over India; but in certain sections there are not only these, but all the home fruits. This section is to the north and northwest. Pears, apples, peaches, plums—in fact, any fruit that can be grown any place in the world can be grown successfully in this favored section of India.

"Why don't missionary ladies do their own cooking?"

The idea seems to be abroad that the reason that missionaries in India do not do more manual labor is because they have a certain dignity that they must maintain; that they would lose caste and influence should they do menial work of any kind. This is quite a mistaken idea. One of the things that a missionary stands for is serving, serving by hands and feet as well as by brain and spirit. The simple reason is that missionaries are employed by the missionary society to do other things. It isn't a question of giving eight hours a day to mission work, but it's a question of giving all the time.

But suppose she hadn't her hands so full of mission work, even then she could not do her own cooking.

Perhaps she might do some of it if she had an up-to-date little kitchen, with linoleum on the floor, if there were a sink and a gas range, and all sorts of lovely pots and pans, but alas! in India there is not even a kitchen. It is a cook-house, and is quite detached from the rest of the house. If she cooked there, the missionary lady would have to keep running back and forth in the hot sun or in the pouring rain of the monsoon. There is no linoleum—only a damp, uneven stone floor, and there is no sink—all the work requiring water is done on the floor by a drain-pipe, and sometimes if the screen gets broken over the mouth of the drain-pipe, toads come hopping in, and sometimes even cobras come squirming through. The Indian cook-house is always dark and smoky. There is no little gas range; just a primitive cooking place made of bricks plastered together. This contains a number of holes in which are inserted grates. Charcoal fires are burning in these little grates. Charcoal has to be fanned and fanned with a black and grimy fan to get it into the glowing stage. Of course a clean fan would do as well, but one never sees a clean fan in an Indian cook-house.

However, do not suppose for a minute that the missionary lady has no responsibility regarding the cooking. She has. She cooks with her nerves and brains. She has to train up the cook in the way he should go, and after he has gotten into the way, she has to walk along by his side, for she must be brains for him for ever and ever. She has to see that he walks in paths of truth and uprightness. She has to keep everything under lock and key, and is apt to lose her keys when she is in the biggest hurry. She is also apt to lose her temper, and feels worse over this than she does when she loses her keys. She has to argue over prices; to fuss over the quality of charcoal consumed. She has to keep her poise when, after ordering something especially nice for dinner, the cook proudly passes around something quite different and not at all nice. She dare not even visit her own cook-house without coughing and making a noise, for fear that she will have a case of discipline on hands that may leave her without a cook. Verily, she is not deceived by the fact that when she enters the cook-house the cook and half a dozen other men who have been playing cards and smoking are respectively standing around like little tin soldiers. She *sees* the hooka or big water pipe standing behind the door, and she *knows* that the bearer has a deck of cards up his sleeves. But even knowing this, all she can do is to meekly transact her business with the cook and go out without saying a word.

However, in spite of all this, the Indian cook is a great comfort. He grows on one. It is surprising how equal he is to emergencies and what really fine things he can make with very few conveniences and often a very stinted allowance of material. There are very few of them who do not take pride in their cooking, and they are never happier than when there are guests in the home and they are having a chance to show off. Nor are they uncleanly, as is often supposed, but they keep their kitchen in such mild disorder that things really appear much worse than they really are.

And now for the last question. Often and often we are asked, "Aren't you glad to get back to the food in America?" My answer is, "Rather," and it is to be spoken with a rising inflection.

We love the American people, and we enjoy the American food, but we think that when it comes to making nice tasty somethings out of almost nothing, America is not in it at all. Nearly every nation in the world can do better.

I hope these recipes will help.

Contents.

CHAPTER I. CURRY

1. Curry Powder. 2. Beef Curry. 3. Chicken Curry. 4. Curry with Curds. 5. Meat Curry with Pastry. 6. Meat Curry with Cabbage. 7. Meat and Split Pea Curry. 8. Massala Fry. 9. Hamburg Steak Curry. 10. Cold Meat Curry. 11. Buffath, or Curry with Vegetables. 12. Buffath of Cold Meat and Vegetables. 13. Fish Curry. 14. Curry from Tinned Salmon, Sardines, or Tuna. 15. Salt Fish Curry. 16. Massala Fry of Fish. 17. Egg Curry. 18. Poached Egg Curry. 19. Eggplant Curry. 20. Curried Stuffed Eggplant. 21. Stuffed Curried Mango Peppers. 22. Mixed Vegetable Curry. 23. Split Pea Curry. 24. Edible Leaves Curry.

CHAPTER II. SAVORY DISHES FROM OTHER COUNTRIES

25. Mulligatawney Soup. 26. Tamales (Mexican). 27. Koorma (Arabian). 28. Spiced Beef. 29. Irish Stew (Old English). 30. Mesopotamia Stew. 31. French Stew. 32. Turkish Stew. 33. All Blaze. 34. Country Captain. 35. Toad in Hole. 36. Minced Meat Patties. 37. Hamburg Cutlets. 38. Potato Patties with Fish or Meat. 39. Beef Olives. 40. Bird Nests. 41. Eggplant Patties. 42. Spanish Steak. 43. Spanish Welsh Rarebit. 44. Kabobs. 45. Char-chiz. 46. Spanish Eggs.

CHAPTER III. SPLIT PEAS OR DAL

47. Split Pea Soup. 48. Dal Soup with Milk. 49. Kidgeri. 50. Armenian Kidgeri. 51. Dal Bhat.

CHAPTER IV. RICE

52. Plain Boiled Rice. 53. Pesh-Pash. 54. Pullao. 55. Beef or Mutton Pullao. 56. Spanish Rice. 57. Pea Pullao. 58. Cocoanut Rice. 59. Meat and Rice Hash. 60. Rice Cutlets. 61. Fried Rice (Parsi).

CHAPTER V. BUJEAS

62. Potato Bujea. 63. Banana Bujea. 64. Summer Squash Bujea. 65. Cabbage Bujea. 66. Radish Bujea. 67. Tomato Bujea.

CHAPTER VI. BREADS

68. Chupatties. 69. Chupatties (Americanized). 70. Prahatas. 71. Potato Puris. 72. White Flour Puris. 73. Sweet Potato Puris.

CHAPTER VII. PICKLES AND CHUTNEYS

74. Kausaundi Pickle (Americanized).

CHAPTER VIII. CHUTNEY

75. Lemon Chutney. 76. Apple Chutney. 77. Rhubarb Chutney. 78. Carrot Pickle. 79. Mixed Vegetable Pickle.

CHAPTER IX. MOST EVERYTHING

80. Puff Paste. 81. Cheese Cakes. 82. Banana Stew with Cocoanut. 83. Roselle Jelly. 84. Roselle Sauce. 85. Tipparee Jam. 86. Orange Marmalade. 87. Orange Jelly. 88. Candied Grapefruit Peel. 89. Banana Cheese. 90. Carrot Cheese. 91. Fruit Cheese. 92. Fools. 93. Jellabies. 94. Gulab Jamans. 95. Malpuas. 96. Crow's Nest Fritters. 97. Hulwa. 98. Bombay Hulwa. 99. Turkish Delight. 100.

I.
Curry.

Many regard curry as one of the new things in cookery. This is a mistake. Curry is an old, old method of preparing meats and vegetables. Nor is it an East Indian method exclusively. In all Oriental and tropical countries foods are highly seasoned, and although the spices may differ, and although the methods of preparation may not be the same, nevertheless, generally speaking, the people of all Oriental countries freely indulge in curried food.

MAKING CHAPATIES

However, in India curry reaches its perfection. The people of India since Vedic times have eaten curry and always will. They eat it very, very hot, and Europeans who live in India soon find themselves falling into the habit of eating very hot and spicy foods. Whether it is good for one to eat as much hot stuff as one is expected to eat in India is a disputed point. In moderation, however, curry is not harmful, and is a very satisfactory and appetizing way of preparing scrappy and inexpensive meats. If carefully prepared, everybody is sure to like it. Do not introduce it, however, to your family as a mustard-colored stew of curry powder, onions, and cold meat served in the center of a platter with a wall of gummy rice enclosing it. Most of the family would hate it, and it would be difficult to get them to the point of even tasting it again. Curry, as usually made in India, is not made with curry powder at all. Every Indian cook-house is provided with a smooth black stone about a foot and a half long and a foot wide. There is also a small stone roller. On this large stone, by means of the small stone, daily are crushed or ground the spices used in making curry. The usual ingredients are coriander seeds and leaves, dried hot chilies or peppers, caraway seeds, turmeric, onions, garlic, green ginger, and black pepper grains. All these are first crushed a little and then ground to a paste, with the addition from time to time of a little water.

Now of course no American housewife would want to squat on the floor and grind up curry stuff on a stone, as do the women of India. So I hasten to say that very good curry may be made from curry powder. Curry powder may be obtained from almost any grocer. The best in the market is Cross & Blackwell's.

A good plan, however, would be to make your own curry powder. It is better, much cheaper, and is very little trouble to make.

The following formula is excellent:

1. Curry Powder.

10 ounces of coriander seed;
1 teaspoon of caraway seed;
1 teaspoon of black pepper;
1 teaspoon of red pepper;
6 teaspoons of turmeric;
4 tablespoons of flour;
1 teaspoon of cloves;
4 teaspoons of cinnamon;
Seeds of six cardamons.

The coriander and turmeric may have to be purchased at a drug store. Buy as many of the spices ground as you can, and grind the others in a small hand-mill or coffee-mill. Sift together three or four times and dry thoroughly in an expiring oven. Put in air-tight bottles. A pound of meat will require about two teaspoons of this mixture. If not hot enough add more red pepper.

Coriander.—You will note that coriander is the chief ingredient of curry powder. Coriander is used extensively in flavoring throughout the East. It can be grown any place, however. The seed can be obtained from any large florist. It grows rank like a weed. The leaves are delicious as a flavoring for meats and vegetables. A patch of this in your vegetable garden will repay you, as many a bit of left-over can be made very tasty by using a little of the finely minced leaf. The seeds are useful in many ways.

Fresh Cocoanut is another ingredient frequently used in making curries. This gives a delicious flavor and also adds greatly to the nutritive value. A cocoanut paste is prepared by a very elaborate process in the Indian cookhouse, but in this country we are not only confronted by the problem of living on our so many dollars a month, but also by the equally great one of living on twenty-four hours a day. So we will pass the method of preparing cocoanut by with the suggestion that you buy your prepared cocoanut. Baker puts up an excellent preparation of fresh cocoanut with the milk. This comes in small tins at ten cents a tin.

Making curry is a very elastic method. Much depends upon the taste of the individual. Some think a teaspoonful of prepared mustard or Worcestershire sauce a great improvement.

Always get cheap cuts of meat for curry. The hock or heel of beef makes perhaps as fine curry as any other cut.

There are many different kinds of curries. Some are so hot that the consumer thereof may feel that he is the possessor of an internal fiery furnace. Some are mustard-colored, some are almost black, some are thin and watery, some are thick, some are greasy, and some would be quite impossible for America.

Onions are always used in making curry, but do not let this discourage any one who does not like onions. One reason that onions are so unpopular is that so often they are improperly cooked. In making curry onions should be cooked until they are perfectly soft. Indeed they should be reduced to a pulp. This pulp helps thicken the curry gravy, and many people who claim that they cannot eat onions really enjoy them without realizing what they are eating.

The recipes which follow are all practical, inexpensive, delicious, and thoroughly reliable.

2. Beef Curry.

Cut a pound of fresh beef into bits. Any cheap cut does well for this. Slice an onion very thinly, and fry together in a dessert-spoonful of fat of any kind, the meat, onion, and two teaspoonfuls of curry powder. When they are nicely browned add several cups of water and simmer gently until the meat is very tender and the onion has become a pulp, thereby thickening the curry gravy. This requires long, slow cooking. More water may be added from time to time. If one has a fireless cooker, it should always be used in curry making. Serve with rice prepared according to taste. In India, curry and rice are always served in separate dishes. The rice is served first and the curry taken out and put over it. Usually chutney (Chapter VIII) is eaten with curry and rice.

3. Chicken Curry.

Cut a chicken up any way you like and fry it with one thinly-sliced onion and the curry powder. The amount of curry powder will of course depend on the size of the chicken. Fry together until the chicken is nicely browned, then add water and simmer until chicken is tender. Remember always to reduce the gravy by slow cooking until it is somewhat thickened by the onion pulp. A couple of sliced tomatoes fried with the chicken, onion, and curry powder is much liked by some—not only in chicken curry, but in all curries.

4. Curry With Curds.

This curry is prepared a little differently. Place in a deep dish one pound of beef or mutton or any kind of meat. Cover with thick curds of milk. These curds should not be too sour. Also add a green mango pepper thinly sliced, and if desired a clove of garlic, finely minced. Let stand in the curds for a couple of hours. In the meantime fry an onion and two teaspoonfuls of curry powder together. When nicely browned add the curd mixture. Cook over a slow fire until meat is tender. Cold sliced meat is very good prepared this way. In this case cook the onions thoroughly before adding the curd mixture. The meat should be cut in small pieces.

5. Meat Curry with Pastry.

Prepare the curry as in No. 1, adding the dumplings after the meat is tender. For the dumplings, mix half a cup of flour into a stiff dough with water. Add a little salt, and roll out very thin. Cut in two-inch squares. Some like a little fresh cocoanut and cocoanut milk added to this curry.

6. Meat Curry with Cabbage.

Half a pound of meat is plenty for this very hearty and inexpensive dish.

Fry the onion, curry powder, and meat together in the usual way. When nicely browned, add several cups of thinly-shredded or sliced cabbage. Cover with water and simmer slowly until all are tender. Just before serving acidulate. In India, tamarind juice is always used for this purpose, but lemon or lime does very nicely. Carrots or turnips may be used the same way and are excellent. Eat with or without rice. Usually this curry is eaten with chupatties (No. 69).

7. Meat and Split Pea Curry.

Cut a half pound of beef or mutton into small bits and fry as usual with onions and curry powder. When nicely browned add a cup of split peas which have been soaking for several hours. Simmer all together in plenty of water until the meat and peas are tender. Serve with rice.

8. Massala Fry.

This is not really a curry, but is an excellent way of preparing tough round steak.

Mix two teaspoonfuls of curry powder into a half cup of flour, and pound by means of a saucer into a pound of round steak. Fry the steak with a sliced onion until quite brown. Then add a little water and simmer until the meat is tender. The gravy should be little and rich. Do not cut the meat. This is a fine casserole dish.

9. Hamburg Steak Curry.

Fry together a pound of hamburg steak, a cup of minced onions, and two teaspoonfuls of curry powder. When these are quite brown simmer with a little water until onions are soft. This can either be served rather dry or with plenty of gravy. In the latter case, serve with rice or kidgeri (No. 49). A teaspoonful of Worcestershire sauce is a help to this curry. This curry is very nice and is quickly made. Made dry, a little jar of it taken to a picnic or on a trip will be found very useful, as it keeps for days. Indeed, all curried meats keep longer than meats prepared in other ways. Hamburg steak curry makes fine sandwiches.

10. Cold Meat Curry.

Any kind of cold meat may be made into curry. Fry onions and curry powder together until nicely browned. Then add enough flour to thicken, as in making gravy. Then add water or cocoanut milk. When gravy has thickened, add cold meat. Simmer slowly for a while. This curry is not so tasty as those made from fresh meat, and it is well to add a teaspoonful of Worcestershire sauce.

11. Buffath, or Curry with Vegetables.

Fry one-half pound of meat, finely diced, with onion and curry powder. Add a little water from time to time, so that the meat will be tender and the onions soft. Then add two teacupfuls of water. As soon as water boils add a cupful of sliced radishes, potatoes, carrots, or any vegetables that will not mash. Cook slowly together until vegetables are soft. In India this curry is always acidulated, but that is not necessary. It is a good plan, however, to always serve sliced lemon with all curries, as some prefer them sour.

12. Buffath of Cold Meat and Vegetables.

Prepare a sauce or gravy, as in No. 10. Add cold meat and any left-over cold vegetable. Simmer gently together for a little while. Do not have too much sauce.

13. Fish Curry.

Fish curry is usually made with cocoanut milk instead of water, but this is not necessary. It should always be acidulated.

Prepare a sauce, as in No. 10, using, if preferred, cocoanut milk instead of water. Also add a little finely-minced garlic and green peppers. Put the raw fish in this and simmer together until the fish is cooked. Serve with rice. Spanish rice is excellent with fish curry. (No. 56.)

14. Curry from Tinned Salmon, Sardines, or Tuna.

Prepare a sauce as in No. 10, using cocoanut milk and a little grated cocoanut. Also add a tiny bit of thinly-sliced green ginger, garlic, and chili pepper. Pour over the fish, and serve with rice and sliced lemon.

15. Salt Fish Curry.

Cut the salt fish into rather small pieces, and soak until no longer very salty.

While it is soaking, fry in plenty of oil or crisco one bunch of green onions, cut up tops and all, a teaspoonful of curry powder, and three half-ripe tomatoes. The tomatoes may be dipped in batter or crumbs. When these are fried add the salt fish. Simmer together for a while. Serve with rice. Eggplant is excellent in this curry instead of tomatoes.

16. Massala Fry of Fish.

Make a paste of flour and water and two teaspoons of curry powder and a little salt. Dip the fish in this curried paste, and then dip again in bread or cracker crumbs. Fry in the usual way. This is a delicious way of preparing any kind of cutlets or chops. In fact, any kind of meat may be fried in the same way.

17. Egg Curry.

Fry a sliced onion with a teaspoonful of curry powder; then add a little flour for the gravy. When this is mixed quite smooth, add a teacup of water or milk or cocoanut milk. Cook until it thickens, then add six hard-boiled eggs. Cut in halves lengthwise. Serve with rice.

18. Poached Egg Curry.

Prepare the curry as for No. 17. When gravy begins to simmer, poach the eggs in it.

19. Eggplant Curry.

Cut round slices of eggplant. Remove the outer rind, dip each slice in batter and fry.

Make the curry sauce in the usual way. When it thickens, carefully put in the eggplant; simmer gently together until the vegetables are well cooked. This is excellent made with half-ripe tomatoes. In each case it is a fine meat substitute. Always serve with rice.

20. Curried Stuffed Eggplant.

Make a curry mince as for No. 9. See that when the meat is cooked there is plenty of liquid. Thicken this mince and gravy with bread crumbs and let stand. Cut the eggplant in half lengthwise, and steam or bake in a very slow oven. When about half cooked, scoop out the center of about each half. Be careful to save the vegetable that you scoop out and mix it with the curry and breadcrumb mixture. Stuff the eggplant shell with this mixture, cover the top with crumbs, and bake. Excellent either hot or cold. A half pound of meat is enough to nicely stuff one eggplant.

21. Stuffed Curried Mango Peppers.

To prepare the mango peppers for stuffing, cut off the tops and remove the seeds. Let stand in salt water until required. Then prepare plenty of rice according to No. 52. Keep in a warm place until required.

Fry Hamburg steak with onion and curry powder according to No. 9. A pound of steak will be plenty for a nice big dish of peppers. Use no water in this mince, but when the meat and onions are partially fried add a cupful of the boiled rice, and mix all together. Stuff the peppers with this mixture of rice and meat.

Put in a roaster and cover with tomato sauce. This sauce may be made from any tinned tomato soup, diluted and more highly seasoned, or it may be made from stewed tomatoes from which the seeds and skins have been removed. Make sauce a little thick. Bake very slowly or steam. Serve with the remainder of the rice.

This is such a hearty dish that one needs prepare nothing else to be served with it.

22. Mixed Vegetable Curry.

All vegetables such as peas, beans, potatoes, carrots, etc., make excellent curry. They may be either freshly prepared or left-overs.

Fry them all together with plenty of onions in a little crisco; add as much curry powder as is desired. If tomatoes are not used, acidulate a combination of tomatoes, eggplant, and peppers. Makes a fine curry. These vegetable curries are usually eaten with chupatties (No. 69).

23. Split Pea Curry.

Soak the peas for two or three hours. Fry in the usual way the onion and curry powder. A teaspoonful of curry powder is enough for a cupful of soaked peas. Mix the peas with the fried mixture. Add plenty of water and cook until the peas are soft enough to mash up into a pulp. Serve with rice. An acid is desired with this curry.

24. Edible Leaves Curry.

This may not sound especially inviting, but in a pinch one might want to try it. The Hindus make curries from many things that we would throw away. Turnip tops, beet tops, radish tops, the young and tender leaves of many jungle plants, also the leaves of many trees; all these are used in making excellent curries. Dandelion greens, spinach, Swiss chard, may all be used in the same way. Prepare the onion and curry powder in the usual way; then add the greens. It is a good plan to add a few potatoes to give body to the curry. Use very little water in cooking. Serve with puris or chupatties. (Nos. 69, 71).

II.
Savory Dishes from Other Countries.

One of the economies in cooking is in the proper seasoning of foods. This is the secret of many an attractive dish made from left-overs, or cheap meats. Every garden should contain a little patch of mint, parsley, sage, coriander, while those who have no garden could easily grow these in window boxes or pots. It is not an extravagance to have on hand plenty of pepper sauce, Worcestershire sauce, kitchen bouquet, and condiments of various kinds. A little of these goes a long way in seasoning, and many a dish which would be very flat and unattractive, by their judicious use is made savory and satisfying.

Garlic is also another seasoning which we use but little, but which is used most extensively throughout the Orient. If properly used it gives a delightful flavor to food. Very little is required. Indeed, often one needs to just rub the sides and bottom of the cooking vessel with the garlic before putting it on the fire. The salad dish may be treated the same way. However, very few would object to a little finely-minced garlic in almost any meat dish, and much in flavor is often gained thereby.

Most of the recipes which follow are quite new to Americans.

25. Mulligatawney Soup.

This is a very famous soup which has been associated with India since the beginning of the English regime. In India it is usually made with chicken, but beef or mutton do very nicely. Stew a pound of mutton. Scrappy mutton, such as neck or ribs, does very nicely. When meat is tender remove from soup.

Fry an onion with a teaspoonful of curry powder. When nicely browned stir into it a tablespoonful of peanut butter; also about a half cup of fresh cocoanut. Mix these up together to a smooth paste and add to the mutton broth. Also pick the mutton from the bones and add to the soup. If the peanut butter does not thicken it sufficiently, thicken with a little flour. Serve with rice. Sometimes the rice is boiled with the mutton, but usually it is boiled separately (No. 52). Lemon juice is usually served with this soup.

26. Tamales (Mexican).

Take a pound of meat. Mutton, chicken, or beef may be used. It must be cut in bits. If the meat has not sufficient fat, add crisco or butter, or whatever one uses. Stew until meat is very tender. Into this soup add a cup of tomato sauce or a cup of boiled and strained tomatoes highly seasoned. Then stir in enough cornmeal to thicken it as for mush. Cook for a few minutes and then turn all into a rice boiler or steamer, and cook until the cornmeal loses its raw taste. When a little cool, add a few raisins, ripe olives, almonds, or peanuts, the latter cut up fine. Make pretty hot with cayenne, and also add a little pimento. Mold into little rolls, and wrap each roll up in corn husks, tying each end, so that the mixture will not escape. Just before eating, steam up again, and serve hot. If one is in a hurry, a dish can be lined with corn husks, the mixture piled in, and corn husks placed over the top of the dish. This is called "tamale pie." If corn husks are not available, it is very good without them. The mixture can either be steamed in a bowl and turned out or it can be sliced cold and fried like mush. It is not necessary to add the raisins, olives, and nuts unless one wants to be rather luxurious.

At the table open up the rolls, remove the husks, and eat with tomato sauce. A good sauce for tamales is made by stewing tomatoes with a little onion and green pepper, straining and highly seasoning. Worcestershire sauce is always good in tamale sauce.

This tamale mixture is fine for stuffing green mango peppers. Indeed, it makes a fine forcemeat for most anything.

27. Koorma (Arabian).

Koorma is usually made from mutton or veal. Mince an onion, a little green ginger, and a tiny bit of garlic and add to a cup of buttermilk. Cover a pound of mutton with this and allow to stand for a while. The mutton may either be fresh or left-over. While the mixture is standing, fry a minced onion; add to it a little turmeric. Turn the buttermilk mixture into this. If the meat is uncooked, also add a little water, so that it may become tender; but this is unnecessary if cold mutton is used. Simmer slowly together until the meat gets tender and the curds dry. At the last a little cocoanut may be added, but this is not necessary. The gravy must be very little and very rich.

28. Spiced Beef.

This is a very nice way of keeping beef if the weather is hot and one has no ice. Cut the meat up, salt a little, turn it into a bowl, and just cover with vinegar. Sprinkle well with mixed spices. When ready to use, fry with tomatoes and onions. This may be kept for several days without ice, even in the hottest weather.

29. Irish Stew (Old English).

Equal parts of meat and potatoes. Half a pound of meat and half a pound of potatoes makes quite a good-sized dish. Cook the meat with a sliced onion in plenty of water until it is almost tender. Then add the potatoes; also a little mint or parsley, a tiny bit of green ginger, and a sprinkle of cinnamon, salt and plenty of pepper. Cook together until all are sufficiently cooked. At the last, if mutton has been used, add half a cup of milk. Thicken a little if desired, only perhaps it is best to cook it until potatoes begin to break, thickening it in that way.

30. Mesopotamia Stew.

Equal parts of meat and string beans. Fry together with or without an onion. When quite brown but not hard, season well in any way liked. In Mesopotamia, of course it is made very hot. Cover with water and cook slowly until beans are soft and meat is tender. Less meat may be used. Beans and meat should both be cut up fine for this stew.

31. French Stew.

Take a pound of beef cut in small pieces and fry it until brown. Remove and fry in the same pan the following vegetables: Three small radishes, three small carrots, three small onions, half a dozen potatoes, a little green ginger, a green chili or two, and three or four mint leaves. The ginger, chili, and mint leaves should be finely minced, but slice the other vegetables. When the vegetables are nicely browned, remove, make a little gravy in the pan; pour this gravy over the meat, add the vegetables, and cook very slowly together until the meat is tender. If liked, it may be made with only potatoes and onions and meat.

32. Turkish Stew.

Fry a pound of meat cut in small pieces. Remove from the pan. In the same pan fry eggplant, thinly sliced and rolled in batter and crumbs. Season as desired. Put a layer of the fried eggplant and a layer of the fried meat in a cooking vessel. Add a little water, and cook very slowly until meat is tender.

33. All Blaze.

This is an old English dish, and is fine for the fireless cooker. Mutton is best for this dish. One pound of mutton, cut in bits, one-half pound of potatoes (quartered), peas, beans, onions, carrots, or any vegetables one may have on hand. Put a layer of potatoes at bottom of the pan, then a layer of meat, then a layer of mixed vegetables. Repeat this, sprinkling salt and pepper over each layer and a little drippings. Put in a vessel with a very tight-fitting lid, so that no steam will escape, and steam or bake slowly for three or four hours.

34. Country Captain.

This is another English dish, and is a great favorite with the Indian cooks. Chicken is always used in India, but veal or mutton will do nicely. Cut up the meat, slice four or five onions in rings, and set aside. Fry the chicken quickly over a hot fire, then fry the onions. With the onions fry some green chilies and a little green ginger; add a cup or two of water and stew until chicken is tender. Do not thicken the gravy to this. Sprinkle fried onions over the platter when it is ready to serve.

35. Toad in Hole.

Make a batter just as you would for pancakes. Melt some butter or crisco in a baking dish and pour in half the batter. On this place a mixture of meat, potatoes, and onions prepared as for No. 29. Pour over this the remainder of the batter and bake or steam.

36. Minced Meat Patties.

Prepare the mince according to No. 9. Make a piecrust, not too rich. Roll out paste, cut out in circles about three inches in diameter. Put in each of these circles a tablespoonful of the curried mince, and turn over, pressing the edges closely together. Fry or bake.

37. Hamburg Cutlets.

Take a pound of Hamburg steak, a minced onion, a minced mango pepper, a leaf or two of mint or coriander, a little salt and pepper, and very few bread or cracker crumbs. Mix all together, mold in little oblong cakes, dip in a thin batter made of flour and water, and then in crumbs. Fry in fat or oil.

38. Potato Patties with Fish or Meat.

Take equal parts of cold mashed potatoes and flour. Work together into a paste and roll out in circles about four inches in diameter. Place in each of circles a spoonful of salmon or tuna; season rather highly, press edges together, and fry. Fine way to use cold mashed potatoes. Curried mincemeat may also be used for the filling.

39. Beef Olives.

Have the butcher cut a very thin round steak either of beef or veal. Cut this in pieces about three inches square, and pound with a saucer about a dessert-spoonful of flour into each of these pieces. Make a highly-seasoned forcemeat of breadcrumbs and onions and a little minced bacon. Place a spoonful of the stuffing on each square of meat, and roll in the form of a sausage. Wrap each roll with cord and tie. Fry the rolls, then remove and make a gravy in the pan. When gravy is made, add the rolls and stew gently until the rolls are tender.

40. Bird Nests.

Stew a pound of boiling meat with two sliced onions until the meat is tender. Remove the meat and onions, and when cold pass through the meat grinder. Season rather highly, add egg and breadcrumbs, and work all together as though for cutlets. If flour is worked well into it, no egg or crumbs will be required.

Boil six eggs until quite hard. When cold, remove the shells. Enclose each egg in the meat mixture. Roll in a thin batter, then in crumbs, and fry. When nicely browned, cut with a sharp knife through the center of each egg. Place on a platter, and pour over all a gravy made from the broth in which the meat was boiled. This makes twelve birds' nests.

A very attractive and delicious salad can be made by using veal or chicken instead of beef. The yolks of the eggs may be removed and deviled or highly seasoned. Serve with mayonnaise dressing instead of gravy.

41. Eggplant Patties.

Take two medium-sized eggplants, steam or bake until tender; then cut lengthwise into halves. Scoop out the pulp, cut the pulp in small bits and set aside. Keep the skins for the patties. Mince an onion, brown it in oil or crisco. When nicely browned, add a quarter of a pound of either cold or raw minced meat, a little green mango pepper, and the pulp which was removed from the eggplant. A little Worcestershire sauce or piccalilli improves this considerably. Fill the empty shells with this mixture. Cover with crumbs and bake. Large ripe cucumbers are good prepared the same way. Only they should be peeled before steaming, and the seeds should be carefully removed. If a gravy could be made of stock and poured over the patties it would be liked by many.

42. Spanish Steak.

Pound thoroughly by means of a saucer a half cup of flour with a pound of round steak. Then over a hot fire quickly fry the steak and remove.

In the same pan fry two good-sized onions, thinly sliced, and half a dozen good-sized tomatoes and one large mango pepper. If the pepper is mild, add cayenne pepper. When the onions begin to get soft and the tomatoes to dry, add the meat. Cook very slowly until meat is tender.

One can use canned tomatoes very nicely for this. Cook onions and tomatoes and peppers together, with plenty of oil or crisco until they begin to thicken. Then add the meat. This is also a very satisfactory way of reserving cold steak or any kind of cold meat. After the tomato and onion mixture is well cooked, add the cold meat and heat up all together.

43. Spanish Welsh Rarebit.

Fry in plenty of oil or butter or crisco a large sliced onion. When onion is partly done, add a tin of tomato soup or a cupful of stewed strained tomatoes. Cook for a little while together, then add half a pound of sharp cheese, three or four pimentos, and a small tin of mushrooms; also add a tablespoonful of Worcestershire sauce. Cook all together slowly for a while, then pour over toast or crackers. This is also called "rinktum ditty."

44. Kabobs.

This is a very popular dish among the Mohammedans. Kabobs are usually cooked by the roadside and served piping hot to pedestrians. They are also cooked on the platform of railway stations and handed out to passengers on the train. Season a pound of minced meat with pepper and salt or any desired spices. Mix with a little flour to hold together. Make in the form of sausages by pressing around iron pins. Roast over a hot fire. These are delicious cooked at picnics. One can easily purchase the iron pins or have them made. They are usually about a foot long and a quarter of an inch thick. If the meat is fat they easily slip from the pins; if it is lean, it is best to grease the pins first.

45. Char-chiz.

Fry together a cup of Hamburg steak, a cup of sliced tomatoes, a cup of minced onions, and a cup of minced peppers. After they have fried until dry, add a cup of water and simmer all together for a while. Make quite hot and serve with boiled rice.

46. Spanish Eggs.

Fry the desired number of eggs very lightly in bacon fat. Just before removing from the pan pour over them a sauce made by adding a tablespoonful of Worcestershire sauce to any good catsup. Heat hastily together and serve. This is a fine meat substitute.

III.
Split Peas or Dal.

Split peas, or "dal," as they are called in India, belong to the lentil family. There are three kinds—the green, which very much resembles an ordinary dried pea; the yellow, and the red. In this country we only see two kinds—the green and the yellow. The red are more frequently seen in India, and have a more delicate flavor.

Lentils are an old, old food. We read of Esau selling his birthright for a mess of red pottage, or a mess of red dal. Then later we read of the Hebrew children refusing to eat the king's meat, and growing rosy and fat on their daily portion of lentils.

Lentils are rich in protein. About twenty-five per cent of their food value is protein. They are richer in protein than beans, and are more digestible.

During Lent in the early days of the Roman Church, lentils were the chief article of food, because of meat being forbidden. Because of this the name lentil was given to them.

Split peas are used universally throughout India. Several recipes have already been given (Nos. 23 and 7), but a few others will be noted.

47. Split Pea Soup.

Soak a cup of peas over night and boil in three cups of water. Cook until peas are soft, then mash them quite smoothly. Then dilute with stock. This stock may be made from bones and cold meat or fresh meat. Fry an onion and add to the soup, and when ready to serve add minced mint leaves and little squares of toast, fried very crisp.

48. Dal Soup with Milk.

Prepare the dal as above, except instead of diluting with stock dilute with milk.

49. Kidgeri.

First soak a cup of split peas for about three hours. Then put them on to stew with two whole onions. When about half done add a cup of rice. The water must be about two inches above the split peas and rice. Cook until rice and peas are soft and the water is absorbed. Pour over all some melted butter or crisco. Usually kidgeri is served with poached eggs. Sometimes eggs are hard-boiled and sliced over the kidgeri after it is dished.

50. Armenian Kidgeri.

Soak a cup of split peas for several hours, then fry with two thinly-sliced onions and a cup of rice. When slightly brown, cover with water and boil. The water should be three inches above the peas and rice; also add a little bag of mixed spices. Fry some meat in a separate pan. It may be either beefsteak, Hamburg, or mutton. When rice and peas are soft, place a layer of meat in a dish and cover with a layer of the rice and peas. Repeat until all are used, being careful to have the rice and peas on top. Steam together and serve with cocoanut and fried onions sprinkled over the top.

51. Dal Bhat.

Dal Bhat is the universal breakfast dish all over India. Prepare as for split pea curry (No. 23), but omit the curry powder, if desired.

Often it is prepared by frying minced meat with the onions before the peas are added.

IV.
Rice.

POUNDING RICE.

As a rule rice is badly cooked in the average American home. For this reason last winter when there was a good deal of talk of rice as a substitute for potatoes, very little enthusiasm was felt on the subject, and indeed when one thinks of the tasteless, gummy mess which is so often put before the family, this lack of enthusiasm is not strange. However, rice properly prepared proves quite a formidable rival of the beloved potato, and there are endless ways of preparing it if one only knows how.

In the first place, very few know how to cook just plain boiled rice. Many know that there is a way of preparing it so that when done it will be a fluffy mass of separate grains, but they have no idea how to go about making it look like this.

The process is very simple. Always use the unpolished rice. Rice with a creamy tinge is better than rice with a pearly white tinge, and the long grain is better than the short.

52. Plain Boiled Rice.

For every cup of rice have about eight cups of water. Do not add the rice until the water is boiling briskly. Then throw in the rice, and give it an occasional stir until the water begins to boil again. After that it need not be stirred.

Cook until a grain feels soft when rubbed between the thumb and finger, then turn into a colander. Drain off the water and pour over the rice several cups of cold water. Drain that off, too, and place the rice where it can have moist heat for a while before serving. A good plan is just to leave it in the colander and place it over a pan of boiling water; or a steamer may be used for keeping it warm, or a double-boiler. By this method every grain is separate. Rice served with curry is always prepared in this way. It may be served in place of potatoes with meat, and may also be used as a basis for many inexpensive and attractive dishes, just as macaroni and spaghetti are.

There is one objection, however, to rice prepared in this way. A good deal of the nutritive value is lost down the sink-drain. In India this is not the case, for every ounce of rice water is there carefully saved. It is used in various ways. Usually it is fed to the babies and weaker children. Often it is given to ducks and fowl to fatten them, and sometimes it is put into the curry pot.

There is another method of preparing rice which is almost as satisfactory, and by which all the nutrition is retained. That is by cooking it in a regular rice boiler. Put just enough water over the rice to well cover it. After the water in the lower vessel has boiled a while, if the rice seems a little dry, add more water. Cook until the rice is soft, then turn the fire very low, so that the water in the lower vessel does not boil but retains its heat. Let stand for a while before serving, and the rice will be almost as fluffy and white as though blanched by the cold water process.

53. Baby's Pesh-Pash.

This is the first solid food that babies of English or American parents in India are allowed.

Take about a quarter of a pound of lean mutton and cook until it is perfectly soft. Shred it finely and return to the broth. Cook a tablespoonful of rice in this broth and shredded mutton. Cook slowly and let every grain swell to its utmost. "Babies cry for it, and the doctors pronounce it harmless." It is also very good for the convalescent.

54. Pullao.

Pullao is the most festive dish in India. It stands for all that roast turkey does in this country. At weddings, feasts, and holidays it is the chief dish. Among the Hindustani Christians it is the Christmas dinner. Sometimes it is served with rivers of hot curry flowing over it, but often it is eaten without the curry. In India it is usually made with chicken, but any kind of meat does nicely.

For chicken pullao, take a good fat hen, not too old, cut up and stew until almost tender. Put a little bag of "mixed spices," such as are used in making pickles, on to cook with the fowl. While the fowl is cooking take about a pound of rice and fry it with a few sliced onions and a little butter or crisco. When the chicken is nearly done, add the fried rice and onions to the chicken and chicken broth. Put all in a rice boiler if you have it and cook slowly until the rice is done. Retain the spices. If rice boiler is used there should be at least two inches of broth above the mixture. If you have no rice boiler, but must boil it on the stove, more broth will be required. In the latter case do not cook until it becomes soggy. Cook until the broth is absorbed, then steam.

While the rice is cooking fry a few more onions with a handful of almonds and raisins. When the pullao is ready to be served, pile on a platter, then strew thickly over the pullao the fried onions, almonds, and raisins. Last of all, sprinkle generously with cocoanut.

55. Beef or Mutton Pullao.

Very delicious pullao may be made from the cheapest cuts of beef and mutton. Get about two pounds of beef or mutton, cut in bits. Cook until it is very tender. Boil with this a little bag of mixed spices and two onions. Unless the meat has a good deal of fat, use crisco, or oil. Two cups of rice will be the right amount to use with two pounds of meat. Use the same method that is used in making chicken pullao. Fresh cocoanut is always delicious strewn over pullao, and if curry is used with it, have cocoanut in the curry.

56. Spanish Rice.

Fry 3 onions, 6 tomatoes, 2 peppers or pimentos together. They must all be cut into small bits. In another pan fry a cup of rice in a very little oil or crisco. After the rice has browned a little, add the two together, turn into a rice boiler or steamer and cook until rice is tender. A half cupful of grated or diced cheese is an improvement to this dish. In case tomatoes are not in season, a can of tomatoes, or, better, a large-sized can of tomato soup will do nicely. In that case fry the onions and peppers and rice together. Then add the cheese and tomatoes.

57. Pea Pullao.

Take two cups of cold boiled rice, add to it two cups of freshly shelled peas. Pour over the mixture a half cupful of milk or cream; add a tablespoonful of butter or crisco, and cook in a rice boiler or steamer until the peas are nicely done. A few bay leaves and black pepper grains are an improvement to this dish.

58. Cocoanut Rice.

Take a cup of rice, mix it into half a grated cocoanut. A ten-cent tin of Baker's cocoanut does very nicely if one doesn't care to prepare the fresh cocoanut. Boil the rice and cocoanut together, being sure to add to the water the cocoanut milk. There should be about three inches of liquid above the rice. Color the liquid yellow with a little turmeric; add salt, six cloves, two cardamon seeds, and twelve pepper berries. Cook in a rice boiler or steamer until done.

59. Meat and Rice Hash.

A very nice way of making hash is to use rice instead of potatoes. Take cold meat and gravy and stew together with onion. When the onion is nearly done, add to the broth the rice. A quarter as much uncooked rice as there is meat is a good proportion. Cook all together until rice is thoroughly done. Be sure and have plenty of liquid to start with. This is much better than meat and potato hash.

60. Rice Cutlets.

Left-over pullao or kidgeri or meat and rice hash make fine cutlets. Mold, roll in crumbs, and fry in the usual way.

61. Fried Rice (Parsi).

(A fine dish for a missionary tea.)

Fry a cup of uncooked rice and a cup of brown sugar in a tablespoonful of butter or crisco. Cook until the sugar melts and begins to bubble; then quickly add two cups of boiling water. Simmer over a slow fire, or, better still, in a rice boiler until rice is thoroughly cooked. It can hardly be cooked too much. Remove from the fire, pour over all a half ounce of rose water and stir well. Press in plates and sprinkle well with minced almonds, or any kind of nuts will do. Also add a few cardamon seeds. When cold, cut into squares and serve like fudge. This is a very satisfactory little sweetmeat when one wants a foreign dish. It is easily prepared and very inexpensive.

V.
Bujeas.

Bujeas are always made from vegetables. They are usually eaten with the native bread instead of rice. Here again the everlasting onion is in evidence, for bujeas are always fried with onions. They are made from any kind of vegetables or green tops of vegetables. Potato bujea is one of the most popular.

AN INDIAN PRINCE

62. Potato Bujea.

To a pound of potatoes take two medium sized onions and one green mango pepper. If the pepper cannot be had, use the tops of onions and a little cayenne. Fry the onions, and when nicely browned add the potatoes and peppers. If potatoes are medium-sized, cut each potato in four pieces. Add four tablespoonfuls of water and if hot food is liked, a good sprinkle of cayenne. If more water is needed, add a couple of tablespoonfuls more. Cook very slowly. Use plenty of oil or crisco in frying the onions. This is good with old potatoes, but is best with new ones. Tiny new potatoes are fine cooked in this way. They do not need to be scraped. Just washed thoroughly and cooked whole.

63. Banana Bujea.

Take half a dozen not too ripe bananas, cut them in pieces, and allow them to lie in weak salt water for a while. Slice two green mango peppers and half an inch of green ginger; also cut in tiny bits a clove of garlic. Brown a sliced onion in butter or crisco. Then add the bananas, peppers, etc. When the fruit softens stir in half a cup of cocoanut; any unsweetened kind will do. Cook a few minutes longer.

64. Summer Squash Bujea.

First peel the summer squash. Then cut in very thin slices. Fry an onion and sliced green pepper together; then add the summer squash. Add very little water. Simmer until done.

65. Cabbage Bujea.

Cabbage bujea is made just as other bujeas are, excepting it is usually acidulated. Sometimes fresh cocoanut is cooked with the cabbage and sometimes a little shredded salt fish is added.

66. Radish Bujea.

In India radishes are cooked just as other vegetables, and radish bujea is very popular. Peppers are not used in making this, but the young tender leaves of the radish plant are used instead. While the onion is frying, parboil the leaves, drain them, and add them to the sliced radishes and onions.

67. Tomato Bujea.

This is a fine bujea. One never cares for meat when this is served. Fry a large sliced onion and a mango pepper together until nicely browned. Remove from the pan and fry in the same pan six sliced not too ripe tomatoes. These should be dipped in batter and then breadcrumbs before frying. When tomatoes are nicely browned add onions and peppers. Do not add any water to this bujea. Heat very slowly until well blended.

Eggplant, okra, pumpkin, string beans, cauliflower, in fact most any vegetable may be cooked in this way. One general rule will suffice: Fry the onions first in plenty of crisco or oil. If desired, fry also top of onions. Then add prepared vegetables and a little water. In most bujeas, peppers or pimentos are used. Cook slowly. Vegetables like eggplant had better be soaked in weak salt water before cooking.

GRINDING WHEAT

VI.
Breads.

Bujeas are always eaten with native bread. For these breads the flour is always ground in the home. The mill used is exceedingly primitive. It consists of two large circular stones, one fitting into the socket of the other. By revolving the upper stone over the lower the grain which is poured between the stones is crushed. It is the women of India who do the grinding, and "two women grinding at a mill" is a familiar sight everywhere throughout the land.

The bread made from this home-made flour differs very much from the bread we know. It is not made into loaves, but into little flat cakes, which are baked over coals on a griddle. No yeast is used.

Although India is one of the greatest wheat countries in all the world, the great majority of people in India do not eat wheat bread. They are too poor for that. They eat bread made from the flour of coarser grains. Some of these grains, such as millet and rye, we are familiar with; others are quite unknown to us. Corn and oats are but little used in India.

The bread made from these coarse grains is hard to digest. It is made by simply mixing the flour with water. The dough is then patted into little cakes. The bread made from wheat, however, is much finer, and Europeans living in India soon grow to be very fond of it. Some of the varieties would not be practical in this country. However, a few forms of Hindustani bread are quite easily managed here, and will well be worth a trial.

68. Chupatties.

Take a pound of whole wheat and mix it with water until a soft dough is formed. Knead this well. Put a damp cloth over it, and let it stand an hour or so. Then knead again. Make out into balls, each ball about as big as a walnut. Then roll each ball into a flat cake about as big around as a saucer. Bake these cakes one at a time over a very thick iron griddle that has been well heated. Keep turning them over and over while they are baking. Fold them up in a napkin as they are baked and keep in a warm place. The inside pan of a double boiler is a good place for them. To be properly made these cakes should be patted into shape instead of rolled, and the Hindustani women always do it that way. These chupatties are eaten with bujeas and curries.

69. Chupatties (Americanized).

Make a dough from a pound of whole wheat flour, a half teaspoonful of baking powder, and a little salt. Knead well and let stand. When ready to bake them, divide into balls as big as a walnut. Roll each out, spread a little oil or crisco over it; fold up and roll again. Grease an iron griddle and bake, turning from side to side. These are not actually fried, but the crisco in them and the greased griddle prevents them from getting hard, as they are apt to do if made according to No. 68.

70. Prahatas.

This is a very rich and satisfying form of native bread. Take a pound of whole wheat and make a dough according to No. 68. Divide the dough into eight equal parts and make each part into a ball. Flatten each ball a little and spread with crisco. Double it up and repeat this three or four times; then roll thin and fry. Use as little grease in frying as is possible.

Puris.

Puris are similar in appearance to chupatties, except they are fried instead of baked.

71. Potato Puris.

Equal parts of mashed potatoes and flour, mixed to a paste and rolled very thin. Make each puri about as large as a saucer. Fry as you would fritters. These sound rather expensive, and they do take a good deal of fat; but they are to be eaten without butter. Eat with curry. Nothing else will be needed at a meal where these puris and curry are served, for they are very satisfying.

72. White Flour Puris.

Knead for ten minutes a dough made from a pound of fine white flour and water. Let stand four or five hours. Divide into little balls and roll until they are as thin as paper. Fry as you would fritters.

73. Sweet Potato Puris.

Take equal parts of mashed sweet potatoes and whole wheat. Work together into a soft dough. Roll out into cakes, but not too thin. Fry in as little grease as possible.

VII.
Pickles and Chutneys.

THE SNAKE CHARMER

74. Kausaundi Pickle (Americanized).

This is a very sour pickle. In India it is always made with sliced green mango, but in this country very sour green apples and lemons do very nicely.

Slice thinly four lemons. Sprinkle well with salt. Cover with vinegar, and let stand for about a month.

Slice thinly four very tart apples, two onions, six large sour cucumber pickles, and three large red peppers. After they are sliced mix intimately, then add two tablespoonfuls of ground mustard seed, a little salt, and, if the peppers are mild, a little cayenne pepper; also add two tablespoonfuls of thinly-sliced green ginger and one tablespoonful of finely-minced garlic.

Drain the salt and vinegar from the lemons and add them to the rest of the mixture.

Roast two tablespoonfuls of turmeric until the raw taste is taken away, then mix with it two tablespoonfuls of ground mustard; add to this a cup of salad and a cup of vinegar. Mix well together and pour over the pickles. If there is not enough oil and vinegar to cover it, add equal parts of each until the pickle is well covered.

This pickle is not to be cooked, but it is best to let it stand in the sun for a number of days. If there is no sun, the warming oven would do. It keeps indefinitely, and is very appetizing. It is fine for sandwiches. A little in Spanish steak or curry adds much to the flavor.

CARRYING TIMBER IN RANGOON

VIII.
Chutney.

Chutney is a sort of a combination pickle and preserve. It is usually made rather sweetly and very hot, and is eaten with curry and rice. It is, however, a fine relish with all kinds of meats. In India it is usually made of the sliced green mango; but of course we haven't mangoes here, so we have to use what we can get. Any tart fruit makes good chutney.

75. Lemon Chutney.

Cut a pound of lemons in twelve bits each, and cook in vinegar and a very little salt until the rinds are perfectly tender. Drain.

Dissolve a pound of sugar in a quart of vinegar; put in the lemons and cook until the mixture becomes thick like jam. Then add a teaspoonful of cayenne pepper (or less), two tablespoonfuls of minced ginger, two tablespoonfuls of mustard seed, and a pound of raisins. Mix all together and boil ten minutes longer.

76. Apple Chutney.

Boil together three pounds of sliced apples, two pounds of sugar, and a quart of strong vinegar. When this begins to get like jam, add half a pound of raisins, four teaspoonfuls of finely-minced garlic, two tablespoonfuls of thinly-sliced green ginger, one teaspoonful of red pepper, and one ounce of mustard seed. Let simmer a while, then bottle and expose to the sun. Apricot chutney is delicious made the same way, with the addition of several ounces of apricot pits, blanched and minced.

77. Rhubarb Chutney.

Make just like apple chutney, only use less vinegar. In addition to the raisins and other ingredients, add a teacupful of finely-minced and blanched almonds. This is worth trying. Less red pepper might be used.

78. Carrot Pickle.

Cut the carrots any way that is desired. If they are very small they need not be cut at all. Sprinkle them well with salt and dry them in the sun for three days, being careful not to forget to bring them in at night. For a pound of carrots take a tablespoonful of mustard seed, half a dozen peppers (sliced), two tablespoonfuls of green ginger (sliced), and two garlics (finely-minced). Cover with vinegar. These are excellent.

79. Mixed Vegetable Pickle.

Eggplant, radishes, onions, carrots, peppers, all are largely used in making pickles in India. They are chopped, sprinkled with salt, and dried for several days in the hot sunshine. Mustard seed, turmeric, and minced garlic are usually added. After several days of sunning they are bottled, covered with vinegar which has been boiled, but which has been cooled.

IX.
Most Everything.

Many of the cooks in India make a very simple puff paste.

80. Puff Paste.

Make a dough out of a pound of flour and sufficient water. Knead for fifteen minutes. Roll in a damp cloth and set aside.

After an hour or so knead again. Then add a spoonful of shortening at a time until the dough begins to crack and looks rough.

Roll out in a sheet, cut in four pieces, place one upon the other, roll again, cut in four pieces again. Repeat this four times, then roll it into a sheet, spread it with shortening of some kind, cut in four pieces, and place one over the other. Then roll for the last time. The advantage of this method is that it takes comparatively little shortening and is always light and flaky. It makes a delicious pastry for cheese cakes.

81. Cheese Cakes.

Place two cups of pure milk over the fire and when the milk begins to boil squeeze the juice of a lemon into it. The milk will at once curdle. Drain off the curds. To these curds add the yolks of two eggs, a tablespoonful of butter, a small cup of sugar, and a small cup of ground almonds. Walnuts, pecans, or any other nuts would do all right.

Mix all together smoothly. Line little patty pans with the paste (No. 80), and fill with the curds. Dust powdered sugar over the top and decorate with crossbars of pastry. Bake very slowly.

These cheese cakes are always much in evidence at afternoon teas, garden parties, and all social functions in India.

82. Banana Stew with Cocoanut.

Boil six bananas. To boil bananas do not remove the skins. Just pour enough boiling water over them to cover them. Add a little salt to the water. As soon as the skins crack they are done. Remove and cool. When cool, take off the skins, scrape the bananas a little and split them.

Make a syrup of one cup of sugar and half a cup of fresh cocoanut and half a cup of water. Pour this over the boiled bananas and serve. This dish is much appreciated by the children.

Roselles.

Roselles are a fruit belonging to the sorrel family. The seed is sown in the vegetable garden every year when other seeds are sown. The plants have a vigorous growth. They grow as tall or a little taller than currant bushes. Long before the season is over the bushes are vivid with wine-red flowers. From the waxen petals of these flowers very delicious sauces, jams, chutneys, and jellies are made.

Roselles can be grown any place as easily as tomatoes or cabbage or any vegetable. It would certainly pay any one to make the experiment. The fruit is very rich in pectin, and not only gives a beautiful color when combined with any other fruit, but also adds much to the flavor. Combined with peaches or strawberries, cherries or guavas, or any other fruit that is deficient in pectin, the roselle has very satisfactory results.

When used by themselves a fine jelly is made which is far superior to currant jelly. I am sure any one will feel repaid who gives it a trial. The seeds can be purchased from any large dealer.

83. Roselle Jelly.

Remove the petals of the flower from the seed; then mince finely by running through the meat grinder. To every cup of minced petals add three cups of water. Boil quickly as the color is much better if it does not stand around. After boiling about five minutes it will be ready to strain. Strain and make as any other jelly. In flavor and appearance this jelly can not be surpassed.

84. Roselle Sauce.

Remove petals from the seed, and for every cup of petals take two cups of water. Stew gently for a few minutes, then add a cup of sugar for every cup of fruit. These two things must be remembered if one wishes to get the best results from the fruit. It must be well diluted and it must be cooked quickly, as it is apt to lose its bright color if it stands around.

Tipparees.

Tipparees, or cape gooseberries, are also another fruit which is much neglected in this country. To many they are familiarly known as ground cherries. These are much prized in India, and they really are a fine fruit, which can be grown any place and will more than repay the little time spent in their cultivation. In India the seeds are sown annually. I think in this country it seeds itself for a few years at least, but I am sure better results would be brought about if the seeds were planted every spring.

This berry is unequaled for making jam. If any doubt it, buy ten cents' worth of seed next spring, plant it in your garden. Let the plants grow and spread and in the early fall make jam according to the following:

85. Tipparee Jam.

Husk the fruit and prick each berry. Do not add too much water, as the fruit is very juicy. Cook until fruit is tender, but not broken. For every cup of fruit allow a cup of sugar. Cook rapidly and not too much at a time. It finishes up very quickly. A good plan is to cook only partially, turn onto platters, and expose to the sun as one does any other sun preserve.

Tipparees are fine for making pies and tarts.

86. Orange Marmalade.

This marmalade can be made from oranges or lemons or grapefruit, or by combining the three, or by combining any two of them.

Either slice the fruit very thinly or run it through a meat grinder. For every cup of fruit take three cups of water. Let it stand for twenty-four hours. Then boil it in the same water until the rinds are soft. Let stand another twenty-four hours in the same water. Then measure again and for every cup of mixture take a cup of sugar. The best results are obtained if not over four cupfuls are boiled at a time. Boil rapidly. If citrus fruits are boiled slowly they are apt to grow dark and strong. If oranges are used alone for this marmalade they must be sour. A good combination is four oranges, two lemons, and half a grapefruit.

87. Orange Jelly.

Mince the oranges, rind and all. For every cup of oranges take three of water. Let stand in water for twenty-four hours. Boil until fruit is soft and let stand again for another twenty-four hours. Up to this point the process is exactly like No. 86.

Now drain the juice from the fruit. Acidulate with lemon juice. If six oranges have been used, add the juice of two lemons. To each cup of juice take a cup of sugar. Boil about four cupfuls at a time and boil quickly. It will soon become jelly. A cup of roselle juice diluted is better to acidulate with than the lemon juice. A beautiful ruby jelly is the result.

88. Candied Grapefruit Peel.

Cut the grapefruit peel in sections. About eight pieces to a grapefruit is a good size. Prick each piece and soak for three days. If the weather is very hot, better scald the fruit instead of soaking it. Change water every morning and evening. On the morning of the fourth day boil the skins until they can be easily pierced. Remove them and squeeze them as dry as possible. Place them on a tray and sun them for several hours, or else dry them in an expiring oven. Weigh the peels, and take once and a half their weight in sugar. Make this sugar with water into a thick syrup; then add the peels and boil until they look clear. Take them out and boil the syrup until it is quite thick. Return the peels and stir around and around until the sugar candies over them. Put them to dry in the sun for a day. Orange and lemon peel, watermelon rind, green muskmelons, and almost any kind of fruit can be preserved in the same way.

89. Banana Cheese.

Take a dozen ripe bananas, skin them, and mash them up with a cup of cream of wheat and a cup of sugar; also add a tablespoonful of butter and a little cinnamon. Cook slowly for about three hours in a double boiler. When cold cut as you would cheese. Fine for missionary functions.

90. Carrot Cheese.

Boil a pound of carrots until very tender. Then mash them perfectly smooth. Mix with them a pound of sugar, a tablespoonful of butter, and the juice of a large lemon. Also add a few cardamon seeds. Cook over a slow fire until the mixture hardens into a paste. Add a little more butter just before removing from the fire. Press into shallow pans and cut in neat squares or diamonds like fudge.

91. Fruit Cheese.

Any fruit may be made into a confection which, in India, is called "cheese." The fruit part first wants to be reduced to a pulp. Then take equal parts of fruit pulp and sugar, with as much butter as you feel you dare use. If you feel that you dare not use any, use crisco with salt. Cook down until it becomes a paste that can be cut with a knife. It must cook very slowly. Sometimes when nearly finished nuts are added. In apricot cheese the kernels are used. They must be blanched and minced. Guava cheese is perhaps the finest, as the flavor improves much with cooking.

92. "Fools."

A fool is a drink made of fruit pulp and milk. Mango fool is perhaps the most popular. Fools are always best made of tart unripe fruits. Pare, slice, and stew the fruit until it is quite soft. Strain through a fine sieve or coarse muslin. Add to the pulp as much sugar as is desired and enough water to make it pour easily. Boil for a few minutes and turn into a jug. When ready to drink it, fill the glass about half full of the fruit mixture and then fill with rich milk. Add ice. These "fools" are very nutritious and refreshing. Often in the hot weather one cares for little else.

Hindustani Sweets.

Hindustani sweets are very sweet, very sticky, very greasy, and very dear to the heart of India's children, both old and young. We do not advise a steady diet of these, but it is well to know how some of them are made, as such knowledge always comes in handy when arranging for missionary programs, Oriental booths in bazaars, and at frequent other times.

93. Jellabies (Best Beloved).

Make a batter of one pound of flour and water. Make it just about as thick as you would for pancakes. Cover the vessel tightly and let stand for three days. Then stir in about a half a cup of thick sour milk. Pour a little of this batter into a vessel with a hole in the bottom. In India a cup made from half a cocoanut shell is made for this purpose, one of the eyes in the monkey face at the end being perforated. Fill this cup with batter and let the batter run through a little at a time into a pan of boiling fat. While the batter is running out through the hole keep the hand moving in a circle, so that the jellabies will take the form of pretzels. Fry as you would doughnuts.

In the meantime have a dish of syrup ready. Make this syrup from a pound of brown sugar and water. Cook it until it is about as thick as maple syrup. Keep this syrup in a warm place and as the jellabies fry place each one for a few minutes in the syrup. Remove and pile them on oiled paper until needed. These are sure to make a hit. Be sure and fry them until they are quite brown. If one doesn't want to bother with the batter standing around for three days, they can be made up at once by adding a teaspoonful of baking powder to the mixture and beating it well. The milk must not be too sour in that case.

94. Gulab Jamans.

Take a pound of rice flour. If one cannot obtain rice flour use common flour. Put it in a bowl. Crack into it two eggs, add a little salt, and enough cocoanut and cocoanut milk to make a soft dough. Use a ten-cent tin of Baker's fresh cocoanut for this. Knead well and cover for a little while with a damp cloth. After a while mold this dough into little balls about the size and shape of pecans. You will have to keep your fingers oiled while doing this. Fry them as you would doughnuts. Let stand until perfectly cold.

Weigh them, and for every pound take a quarter of a pound of white sugar. Make this sugar into a syrup. When thick put in the gulab jamans and stir them for a few minutes. When they are well frosted, remove. Spread out on oiled paper. These are really very nice. Any kind of little cakes and nuts can be frosted the same way. The syrup should be allowed to cool a little before the cakes are put in it.

95. Malpuas.

Make a batter of one pound of cream of wheat and water. This batter should be very thick. Let stand two days. Then add a cup of grated cocoanut, a cup of small raisins, two eggs, a cup of sugar, half a cup of curds, and a little flour. Fry as you would pancakes. These are to be eaten cold. These are also very nice to serve at functions. If each one of these little cakes is made the size of a dollar, a large number could be prepared. A heavy aluminum griddle is very nice for frying these, as they would then require but little fat.

96. Crow's Nest Fritters.

Pare and cut in very small strips a pound of sweet potatoes. Steam until a little soft, but not entirely so. Make a batter of flour, two eggs, and water. Put a tablespoonful of batter on a well-greased griddle, then a tablespoonful of the potatoes. Cover these with another tablespoonful of batter. When done on one side, turn. Eat with melted brown sugar and butter or with syrup.

97. Hulwa.

Fry a cupful of cream of wheat in half a cup of butter or crisco. When it begins to have a nutty flavor and to be slightly brown, add three cups of water and one cup of sugar and a few of the small inside seeds of the cardamon. Boil slowly until it forms a thick rich paste. Press into square cake pans and sprinkle over the top minced nuts and also raisins, if desired. Cut in squares like fudge. Very good and wholesome.

98. Bombay Hulwa.

Bombay hulwa is noted all over India. Soak a pound of cream of wheat in enough water to cover it. Let it stand three or four hours. Then rub it through a coarse strong cloth until you get all the starch out. To do this you must keep dipping the cloth in water again and again. Let this water stand until the starch has settled, then pour off the water. Make two pounds of white sugar into a syrup. Boil until it reaches the fondant stage, then add the cream of wheat starch, and keep boiling and stirring until it forms into a lump. Then add about half a pound of butter. Crisco will do as well if salt is used with it. Go on cooking the hulwa until it begins to get so hard that you can hardly manage it. Then add a wineglass of rose water, some blanched and shredded almonds and the little inside seeds of half a dozen cardamons. Delicious and nourishing, but rather expensive.

99. Turkish Delight.

This popular confection is made by a similar method to No. 98, excepting gum arabic is used instead of cream of wheat starch. The right proportion is about an ounce of powdered gum arabic to two pounds of sugar. The butter also is omitted at the last, but the almond, rose water, and cardamon seed are usually added. Press into plates, cut in squares, and roll each square in powdered sugar.

There is an easier way, however, to make it. Melt gum-drops. This is easily done by adding a little water and boiling, or by keeping hot in a double boiler or fireless cooker for a while.

Add the almonds and cardamons and lemon or orange juice if desired. Dust powdered sugar in a square pan. Press in the paste, dust powdered sugar over the top. Cut in squares.

100. Frosted Bananas.

Use rather green bananas for this. Peel, slice crosswise, sprinkle lightly with salt and fry. Be careful to keep them whole and not to burn them. Allow them to get thoroughly cold, then frost as directed for gulab jamans (No. 94).

101. Sujee Puffs.

Make the paste according to No. 80. To make the mince heat a cupful of cream of wheat in a little butter. Do not fry this brown, but heat all through. Stir into this half a cup of dessicated cocoanut, two tablespoonfuls of small seedless raisins, two tablespoonfuls of almonds (blanched and sliced), and the seed of six cardamons. Cook this mixture for a few minutes, then add a cup of sugar and cook for a few minutes longer. This will not be a paste, for no water has been added; so don't think it is not right if it is very crumbly; that is the way it ought to be. Roll the paste out not too thin, cut in circles with a pound-baking-powder tin. Put as much of the sweetmeat as you think you can enclose, fold over, make as fancy as you like, and either fry or bake.

This is a favorite sweet at native weddings.

102. Breadcrumb Balls.

Mix dry breadcrumbs and grated cocoanut together, and a few raisins, too, if liked. Take a cup of sugar and half a cup of water, and boil. When syrup has reached the stage that it forms a hard ball in water, pour over the breadcrumb mixture. Mold as if making popcorn balls. If one likes, these may be rolled in powdered sugar afterward. These are also a very fine sweet for social and missionary functions of all kinds.

103. Sujee Biscuits.

One pound of cream of wheat and one pound of sugar mixed intimately; then add half a cup of lard or crisco and knead awhile. Form into little balls and shape the balls as desired. Usually they are simply flattened out into squares. Bake a light brown. Be careful that they are not crowded in the pan.